Sing With Me in Mandarin

A Fun and Easy Way to Learn Chinese

Patricia Tina Wu, M.A.Ed.

ISBN 978-0-692-30663-5

For more information about *Sing With Me in Mandarin* please contact littlebamboo@gmail.com.

Cover Art by May Yueng

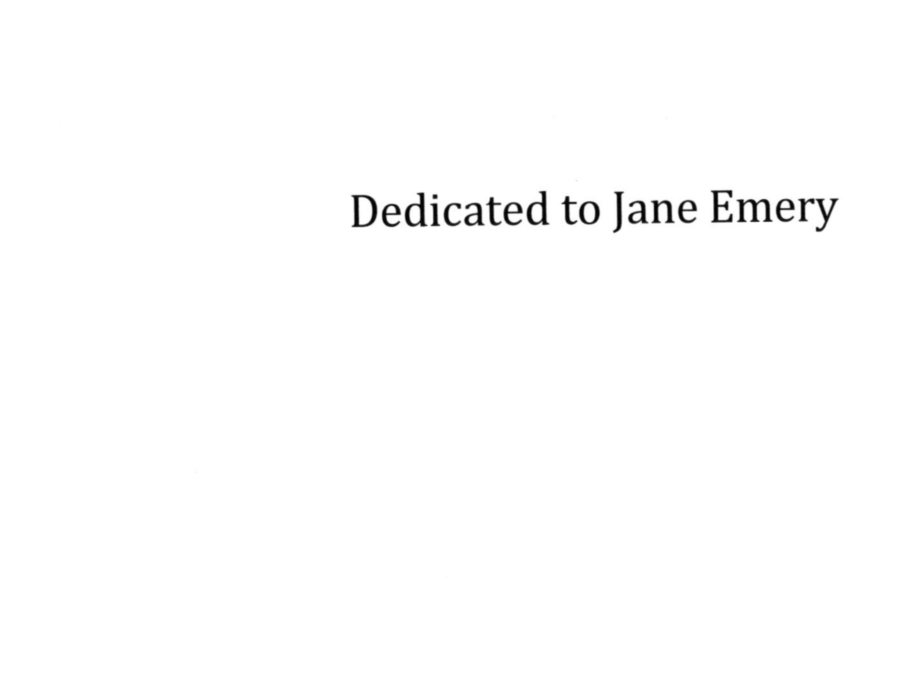

Dedicated to Jane Emery

Contents

Dear Readers,

For many years now I have been teaching Parent and Me music and movement classes using Mandarin Chinese children's songs as a means to teach Chinese. It's a short class, a little under an hour, and we do lots of singing, clapping, dancing, and playing with props and instruments. Parents and children listen to a collection of rhymes and songs at home each week and we recite and sing them together in class. We do crafts, read stories, and practice vocabulary related to the lyrics that we recite and sing.

It's a pretty simple concept, but I am always thrilled by what I see: within a few weeks, quite a few of the toddlers and preschoolers start speaking Chinese! A song may be only memorized and the meaning not fully understood, but what a great start! The language is in their minds and heads! And if they love the songs, it's in their hearts too. Young children acquire a second language effortlessly, especially when it's embedded in music and used meaningfully.

In this book you will find a collection of Mandarin Chinese rhymes and song lyrics that I have used to teach my classes and my own young children. Each rhyme or song lyric comes with pinyin pronunciation, a list of key vocabulary words, and the English translation broken down in a meaningful way.

Along with this book you will find a CD of original recordings to accompany each of the rhymes and songs. The rhymes are recited slowly and the songs are sung either a capella or with simple instrument accompaniment so they are easy to learn.

For parents and teachers I have included some tips and lesson ideas that have worked well in my classes. Parents can easily replicate the activities at home, and teachers can modify the activities for use in their classrooms. I have also included hand motions and activities that go along with the rhymes and songs. Young children learn best when their hands are busy and they are having fun moving around. This is especially true when it comes to learning music and a second language.

Finally, the book contains reference lists of frequently used vocabulary, a pinyin pronunciation guide, and notes explaining how to differentiate the four tones when speaking Chinese.

My children are growing up and I am not teaching much anymore, but I do want to share a resource that has been invaluable to myself as a parent and as teacher over the last decade. So here it is —*Sing with Me in Mandarin*—may it be useful and helpful to you as you embark on the magical journey of teaching and learning Chinese through the remarkable medium of music and song.

Happy Singing!

Tina Lǎo Shī

"Teacher Tina"

Rhymes and Chants

Big Head (#4 on CD)*

Dà tóu dà tóu
大 头 大 头
Big head, big head

Xià yǔ bù chóu
下 雨 不 愁
It rains but you're not worried

Nǐ yǒu yǔ sǎn
你 有 雨 伞
You have an umbrella

Wǒ yǒu dà tóu
我 有 大 头
I have a big head

Big head	dà tóu
Rains	xià yǔ
Worry	chóu
You	nǐ
Have	yǒu
Umbrella	yǔ sǎn

Hand Motions

Rhymes work best with when you include hand motions. Here are my hand motions for this rhyme:

First I stretch my arms out wide for "dà" (big) and then point to my head. (I do this twice.) Then I make raining movements with my fingers. Next I point outwards to indicate "nǐ" (you). After that I pretend I'm holding an umbrella, point to myself for "wǒ" (I) and then hold my arms wide again for "dà" (big) and touch my head with both hands one last time. Have fun!

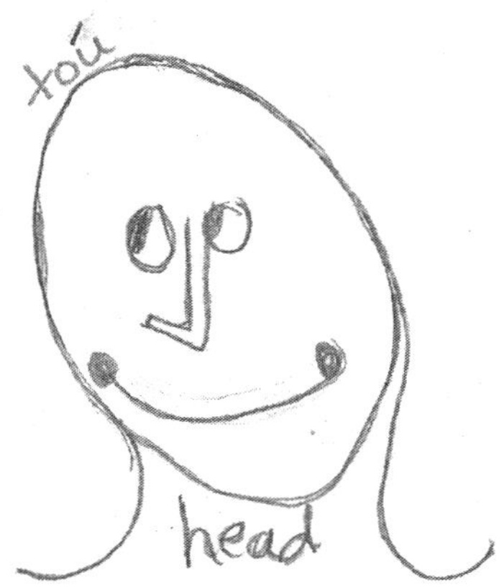

***The number after the title corresponds to the track number on the CD.**

Frog Song (#5)

Yì zhī qīng wā yì zhāng zuǐ
一 只 青 蛙 一 张 嘴
One MW frog one MW mouth

Liǎng gè yǎn jīng sì tiáo tuǐ
两 个 眼 睛 四 条 腿
Two MW eyes four MW legs

Pū tōng pū tōng tiào xià shuǐ (2X)
扑 通 扑 通 跳 下 水
"Plop" "plop" jump into the water

Measure words (MW) come before counted nouns in Chinese. For example, the measure word 只 or "zhī" is placed after the word "one" when saying "one frog".

Frying Eggs (#6)

Chǎo jī dàn chǎo jī dàn chǎo chǎo chǎo
炒 鸡 蛋 炒 鸡 蛋 炒 炒 炒
Fry eggs, fry eggs; fry, fry, fry

Qiē luó bo qiē luó bo qiē qiē qiē
切 萝 卜 切 萝 卜 切 切 切
Chop carrots, chop carrots, chop chop chop

Bāo jiǎo zi bāo jiǎo zi niē niē niē
包 饺 子 包 饺 子 捏 捏 捏
Wrap dumplings, wrap dumplings; pinch, pinch, pinch

Fry	chǎo	
Egg	jī	dàn
Chop(cut)	qiē	
Carrots	luó	bo
Wrap	bāo	
Dumplings	jiǎo	zi
Pinch	niē	

Hand Motions

For the frying eggs portion hold one hand flat with the palm side up for the "pan" while flipping your other hand like a "spatula" over and over against the "pan" hand. It should make a nice slapping sound. For the cutting carrots portion, make one hand a "knife" and the distance from your elbow to the tips of your fingers on the other hand the "carrot" that you chop. For the dumpling portion first make kneading movements with your fingers as if you are wrapping dumplings and then lightly pretend pinch your child at the end of the poem. Toddlers love this rhyme!

Little Leather Ball (#7)

Xiǎo pí qiú xiāng jiāo lí
小 皮 球 香 蕉 梨
Little leather ball, banana, pear

Mǎn dì kāi huā èr shí yī
满 地 开 花 二 十 一
Blooming flowers all over the ground; twenty one

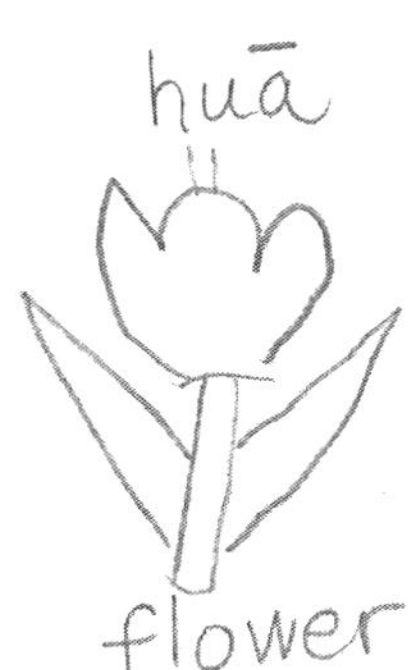

Èr wǔ liù èr wǔ qī
二 五 六，二 五 七
two, five, six; two, five, seven

Èr bā èr jiǔ sān shí yī
二 八 二 九 三 十 一
two eight two nine thirty-one

Teacher Tip: How I Teach This Song

This is a great song to teach numbers and rhythms because it has such a catchy rhyme. For my class I use sticks, eggs, bells, tambourines, drums, and rattles to teach this song. But at home you can use anything that makes a sound. Pots and pans and wooden spoons and/or the bottom of a plastic storage bin and some chopsticks work great. Try singing this song medium, then slow and then fast. Children like sudden changes in tempo and doing so keeps their attention since they don't know what to expect next. This is also a great song to jump rope to!

Little	xiǎo
Leather ball	pí qiú
Banana	xiāng jiāo
Pear	lí
Ground	dì
Flowers	huā
Two	èr
Five	wǔ
Six	liù
Seven	qī
Eight	bā
Nine	jiǔ
Thirty-one	sān shí yī

Little Mouse (#8)

Xiǎo lǎo shǔ shàng dēng tái
小 老 鼠 上 灯 台
Little mouse climbs up the lampstand

Tōu yóu chī xià bù lái
偷 油 吃 下 不 来
Steals oil to eat, can't come down

Jiào mā ma mā bù lái
叫 妈 妈 妈 不 来
Calls "Mom" but Mom doesn't come

Jiào bà ba bà bù lái
叫 爸 爸 爸 不 来
Calls "Dad" but Dad doesn't come

Jī li gū lū gǔn xià lái *
叽 里 咕 噜 滚 下 来
Ji-li-gu-lu rolls on down

*In the CD recording "jī li gū lū" is said twice for emphasis.
(The term "jī li gū lū" is the sound of the mouse rolling.)

Little	xiǎo
Mouse	lǎo shǔ
Up	shàng
Lampstand	dēng tái
Steal	tōu
Oil	yóu
Eat	chī
Call	jiào
Mom	mā ma
Dad	bà ba
No/Not	bù
Down	xià
Come	lái
Come down	xià lái

Body Motions

This popular Chinese rhyme can also be sung (as many rhymes can be). This is a good rhyme to practice direction words, "shàng" (up) and "xià" (down) with your child. First start up on your tiptoes to demonstrate "shàng" (up) and then crunch down really fast to demonstrate "xià "(down). You can also lift your child up and down down or put her on your knees while you are sitting down and pretend your legs are an elevator going up and down.

When singing this song I like to walk on my tiptoes holding my hands curved in front of me like a mouse. Next I pretend to steal some cheese and then call out to Mom or Dad with my hands cupped along the side of my mouth. Finallly, I make a rolling down movement with my arms and fall on the ground. When your little one falls to the ground you can give him a great, big hug!

Little White Cat (#9)

Xiǎo bái māo xiǎo bái māo
小 白 猫 小 白 猫
Little white cat, little white cat

Tā zuò zhe bǐ zhàn zhe gāo
她 坐 着 比 站 著 高
She's taller when she sits than when she stands!

Little	xiǎo
White	bái
Cat	māo
Sit	zuò
Stand	zhàn
Tall	gāo

Still Night (#10) by poet Li Bai

静夜思 李白

This is a very famous Classical Chinese poem!

Chuáng qián míng yuè guāng
床 前 明 月 光
Bright moonlight before my bed

Yí shì dì shàng shuāng
疑 是 地 上 霜
Suspect it's frost on the ground

Jǔ tóu wàng míng yuè
举 头 望 明 月
Lift my head and look at the moon

Dī tóu sī gù xiāng
低 头 思 故 乡
Lower it and think of my hometown

Bed	chuáng
Front	qián
Moonlight	yuè guāng
Bright	míng
Suspect	yí
Ground	dì
Frost	shuāng
Head	tóu
Think	sī
Hometown	xiāng

xīng xīng
star
ZZZzo
yuè liàng
moon

Children's Songs

Butterfly (#11)

by Patricia Tina Wu

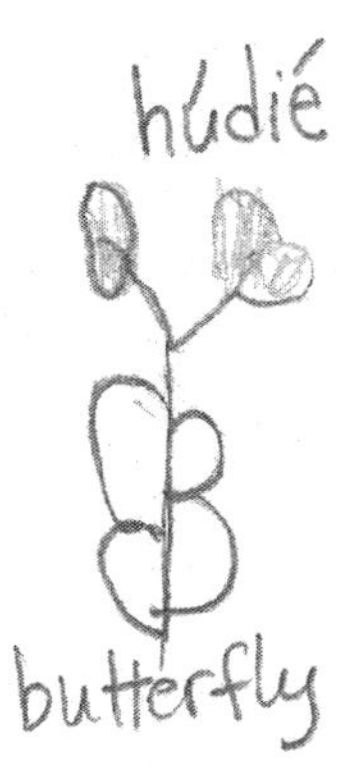

Hú dié hú dié fēi de gāo
蝴 蝶 蝴 蝶 飞 得 高
Butterfly, butterfly, flies so high

Hú dié hú dié fēi de dī
蝴 蝶 蝴 蝶 飞 得 低
Butterfly, butterfly, flies so low

Hú dié hú dié fēi de gāo
蝴 蝶 蝴 蝶 飞 得 高
Butterfly, butterfly, flies so high

Fēi dào zhè lǐ
飞 到 这 里
Flies over here

Butterfly	hú dié
Fly	fēi
High	gāo
Low	dī
Here	zhè lǐ

Teacher Tip

Butterflies are a fun theme to teach. I like to take my students on a pretend butterfly hunt where I hide some decorative paper butterflies and ask the children to hunt for them and place them in butterfly nets as they find them. Then we count up all the butterflies.

Counting Song (#12)

Yī èr sān sān èr yī
一 二 三, 三 二 一
Yī èr sān sì wǔ liù qī
一 二 三 四 五 六 七
Èr sān sì sì sān èr
二 三 四, 四 三 二
Sì wǔ liù qī bā jiǔ shí
四 五 六 七 八 九 十

One, two, three; three, two, one
One, two, three, four, five, six, seven
Two, three, four; four, three, two
Four, five, six, seven, eight, nine, ten

For Number Vocabulary: See *Frequently Used Vocabulary* p.37

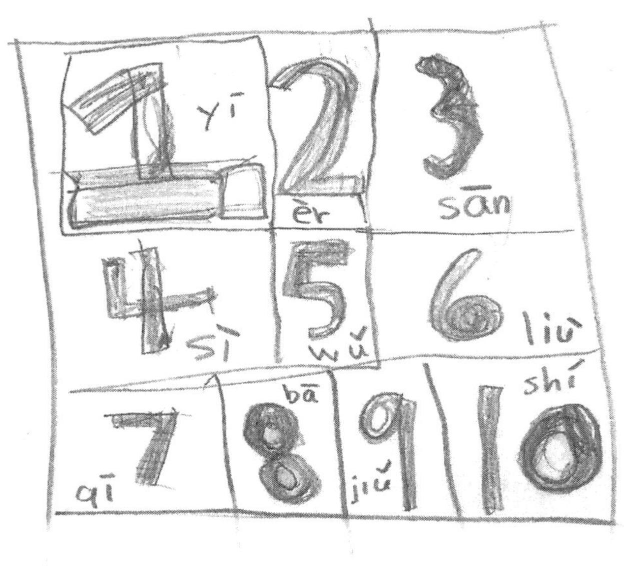

Drop the Handkerchief (#13)

Diū diū diū shǒu pà
丢 丢 丢 手 帕
Drop, drop, drop the handkerchief

Qīng qīng de fàng zài
轻 轻 地 放 在
Lightly put it

Xiǎo péng yǒu de hòu miàn
小 朋 友 的 后 面
Behind a little friend

Dà jiā bú yào gào sù tā
大 家 不 要 告 诉 她(他)
Everyone don't tell her (him).

Kuài diǎn kuài diǎn zhuā zhù tā *
快 点 快 点 抓 住 它(他)
Quickly, quickly, catch it (and him)!

*Repeat this line once.

Drop	diū
Handkerchief	shǒu pà
Lightly	qīng qīng de
Little friend	xiǎo péng yǒu
Behind	hòu miàn
Everyone	dà jiā
Don't tell	bú yào gào sù
Her/him	tā
Quickly	kuài diǎn
Catch	zhuā zhù
It	tā

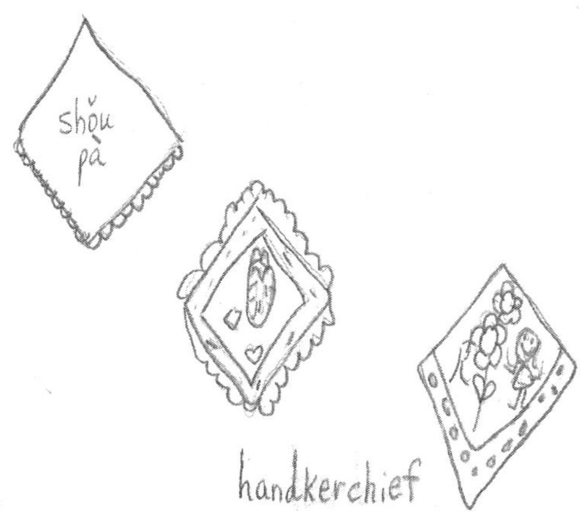

How to Play

Place a handkerchief on the back shoulders of your child. Next make a "sh" gesture with your index finger and see if he notices it or not. Finally, quickly pull the handkerchief from behind him and also "catch" your child by giving him a great big hug.

Another Game

Another way to play this game is similar to how you play Duck Duck Goose. Kids sit in a big circle. One child walks around and drops the handkerchief behind a seated child. The child who just had the handkerchief dropped behind her becomes the "goose" and tries to tag the child who dropped it before that child sits down in her original spot.

Elephant (#14)

Dà xiàng dà xiàng
大 象 大 象
Elephant, elephant

Nǐ de bí zi zěn me nà me cháng
你 的 鼻 子 怎 么 那 么 长
Why is your nose so long?

Mā ma shuō bí zi cháng
妈 妈 说 鼻 子 长
Mama says a long nose

cái shì piào liang
才 是 漂 亮
is what is pretty

Elephant	dà xiàng
Your	nǐ de
Nose	bí zi
Why	zěn me
So	nà me
Long	cháng
Mama	mā ma
Says	shuō
Is	cái shì
Pretty	piào liang

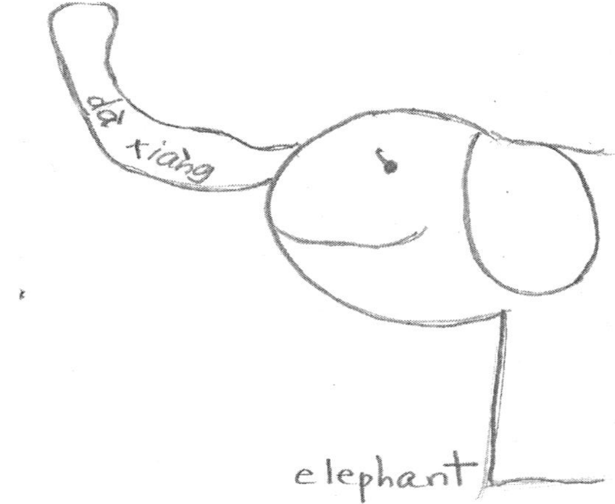

Fast Train (#15)

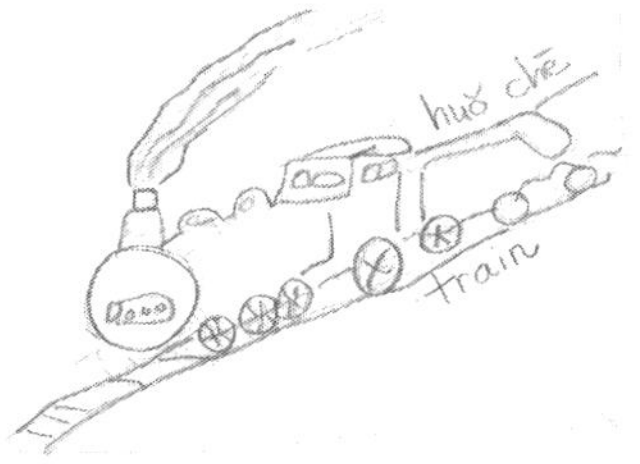

Huǒ chē kuài fēi huǒ chē kuài fēi
火 车 快 飞 火 车 快 飞
Train flies fast, train flies fast

Chuān guò gāo shān fēi guò xiǎo xī
穿 过 高 山 飞 过 小 溪
Passes through tall mountains, flies over small streams

Bù zhī pǎo le jǐ bǎi lǐ
不 知 跑 了 几 百 里
Don't now how many hundreds of miles it has run

Dā dào jiā lǐ dā dào jiā lǐ
搭 到 家 里 搭 到 家 里
Taking the train home, taking the train home

Mā ma kàn jiàn zhēn huān xǐ
妈 妈 看 见 真 欢 喜
I'm extremely happy to see Mommy!

Teacher Tip: Take out the Pots and Pans!

I always try to add noisy manipulatives when I am teaching little ones. For "Fast Train" parents at home can take out wooden spoons, whistles, pots, pans, or anything else that makes a fun sound. In class I like to line up the kids in a line and pretend we are a train. When my own children were young we would march around the kitchen island with instruments or anything that made a joyful noise in hand.

Train	huǒ chē
Fast	kuài
Fly	fēi
Tall	gāo
Pass or cross	chuān guò
Mountains	shān
Small	xiǎo
Streams	xī
Don't know	bù zhī
Run	pǎo
How many miles	jǐ bǎi lǐ
Home	jiā
Mommy	mā mā
Sees	kàn jiàn
Extremely	zhēn
Happy	huān xǐ

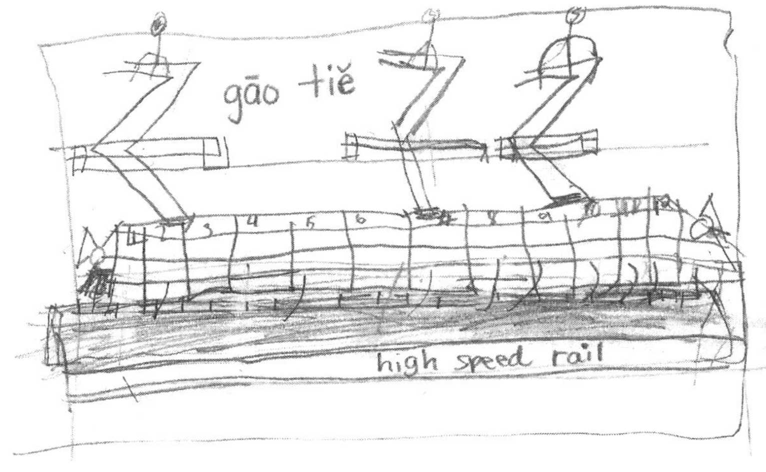

Firefly (#16)

Xiǎo xiǎo yíng huǒ chóng
小 小 萤 火 虫
Little, little firefly

Fēi dào xī fēi dào dōng
飞 到 西 飞 到 东
Fly to the west, fly to the east

Zhè biān liàng nà biān liàng
这 边 亮 那 边 亮
Here shining bright, there shining bright

Hǎo xiàng yí gè xiǎo dēng long
好 像 一 个 小 灯 笼
Looks like a little lantern

Little	xiǎo
Firefly	yíng huǒ chóng
Fly	fēi
West/East	xī / dōng
This side (here)	zhè biān
That side (there)	nà biān
Shiny, bright	liàng
Like, seems to be	hǎo xiàng
Lantern	dēng long

Grandma'sBridge (#17)

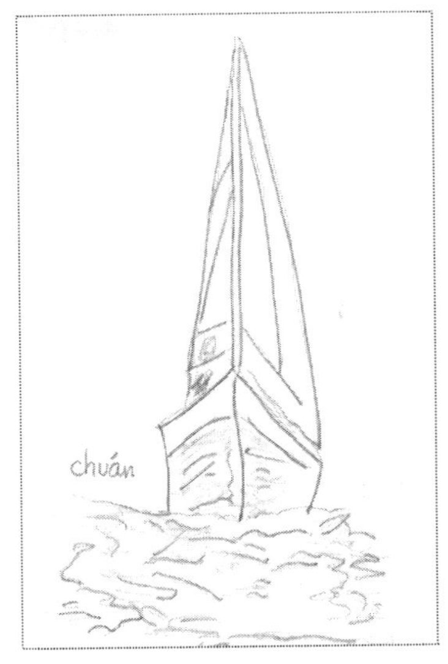

Yáo a yáo yáo a yáo
摇 啊 摇，摇 啊 摇
Rock, rock, rock, rock (a baby)

Chuán er yáo dào wài pó qiáo
船 儿 摇 到 外 婆 桥
Boat rows to Grandma's bridge

Wài pó hǎo wài pó hǎo
外 婆 好 外 婆 好
Grandma hello, Grandma hello

Wài pó duì wǒ xī xī xiào
外 婆 对 我 嘻 嘻 笑
Grandma gives me a smile

Rock	yǎo
Mother's mom	wài pó
Bridge	qiáo
Name....hello	name...hǎo
Laugh, smile	xiào

Teacher Tip

I sometimes use finger puppets depicting family members when teaching this song. I have also constructed a pretend bridge with various IKEA stepstools. Childen take turns walking across the bridge while parents hold their hands to make sure they don't fall down. It sounds very simple but it is really a lot of fun for everyone!

Harp Lullaby (#18)

By Patricia Tina Wu

Shuì jiào shuì jiào
睡 觉 睡 觉
Sleep, sleep

Xiǎo bǎo bèi shuì jiào
小 宝 贝 睡 觉
Treasured one, sleep

Try This at Bedtime

"Brahms Lullaby" is such a famous song that I composed super simple lyrics to accompany its melody so children can learn it right away.

The beautiful harp you hear in this song sounds peaceful and relaxing.

Try playing it on repeat as your little one is drifting off to asleep.

Sleep	shuì jiào
Little treasured one	xiǎo bǎo bèi

Head, Shoulders, Knees and Toes (#19)

Tóu er jiān bǎng xī jiǎo zhǐ
头 儿 肩 膀 膝 脚 趾
Head, shoulders, knees, toes

Xī jiǎo zhǐ xī jiǎo zhǐ
膝 脚 趾, 膝 脚 趾
knees, toes; knees, toes;

Tóu er jiān bǎng xī jiǎo zhǐ
头 儿 肩 膀 膝 脚 趾
Head, shoulders, knees, toes

Yǎn ěr bí hé kǒu
眼 耳 鼻 和 口
Eyes, ears, nose and mouth

Head	tóu er
Shoulders	jiān bǎng
Knees	xī gài
Toes	jiǎo zhǐ
Eyes	yǎn jīng
Nose	bí zi
Mouth	kǒu

Little Sister Carries a Doll (#20)

Mèi mei bēi zhe yáng wá wa
妹 妹 背 着 洋 娃 娃
Little sister carries her doll

Zǒu dào huā yuán lái kàn huā *
走 到 花 园 来 看 花
Walks to the garden to look at flowers

Wá wa kū le jiào mā ma
娃 娃 哭 了 叫 妈 妈
Little one cries and calls to Mom

Shù shàng xiǎo niǎo xiào hā ha
树 上 小 鸟 笑 哈 哈
Bird on tree smiles and laughs ha ha

*For boys, you can replace the first two lines with the following words:

Dì di ná zhe xiǎo shū bāo
弟 弟 拿 着 小 书 包
Little brother carries a little book bag

Zǒu dào huā yuán lái kàn māo
走 到 花 园 来 看 猫
Walks to the garden to look at the cat

Little sister	mèi mei
Little brother	dì di

("Little sister" and "little brother" are terms of endearment sometimes used to refer to young children, not just your own biological siblings)

Carries	bēi (on back)
	ná (by hand)
Doll	yáng wá wa
Little	xiǎo
Book bag	shū bāo
Cat	māo
Walk	zǒu
Garden	huā yuán
Look	kàn
Flowers	huā
Child/baby	wá wa
Cry	kū
Calls mom	jiào mā ma
Trees	shù
Little bird	xiǎo niǎo

Sing This Song at Naptime

This is a perfect song to sing to your children at naptime bedtime. If the song is too difficult to learn at first, you can always repeat the first line over and over or just hum the melody as your child falls to sleep.

Little Swallow (#21)

Xiǎo yàn zi chuān huā yī
小 燕 子 穿 花 衣
Little swallow wearing colorful clothes

Nián nián chūn tiān lái dào zhè lǐ
年 年 春 天 来 到 这 里
Every spring you come here

Wǒ wèn yàn zi nǐ wèi shà lái
我 问 燕 子 你 为 啥 来
I asked the swallow, why do you come?

Yàn zi shuō zhè lǐ de chūn tiān zuì měi lì
燕 子 说 这 里 的 春 天 最 美 丽
Swallow said, the spring here is most beautiful

Swallow	yàn zi
Wears	chuān
Colorful Clothes	huā yī
Year	nián
Spring	chūn tiān
Come	lái
Here	zhè lǐ
Beautiful	měi lì

Looking for a Friend (#22)

> **Teacher Tip**
>
> This song is fun to sing in pairs with a friend. Children can use one hand to make a shade for their eyes as if looking out for someone, salute with a slight bow, shake hands, and then wave goodbye.

Zhǎo ya zhǎo ya zhǎo ya zhǎo
找 呀 找 呀 找 呀 找
Look for, look for, look for

Zhǎo dào yí gè hǎo péng yǒu
找 到 一 个 好 朋 友
I found a good friend

Jìng gè lǐ ya wò wò shǒu ya
敬 个 礼 呀 握 握 手 呀
Salute and shake hands

Nǐ shì wǒ de hǎo péng yǒu
你 是 我 的 好 朋 友
You are my good friend

Zài jiàn
再 见
Goodbye!

Look for (find)	zhǎo	
One + MW	yí	gè
Friend	péng	yǒu
Salute	jìng	gè lǐ
Shake hands	wò	shǒu
You are	nǐ	shì
Goodbye	zài	jiàn

Mommy's Eyes (#23)

Měi lì de měi lì de
美 丽 的 美 丽 的
Beautiful, beautiful

Tiān kōng lǐ
天 空 里
In the sky

Chū lái le guāng liàng de
出 来 了 光 亮 的
Appear shiny bright

Xiǎo xīng xīng
小 星 星
Little stars

Hǎo xiàng shì wǒ mā ma
好 像 是 我 妈 妈
They look like my mommy's

Cí ài de yǎn jīng
慈 爱 的 眼 睛
Loving eyes

Hand Motions

First wave your hands overhead from side to side. Then open and close your fists to show stars sparkling. Next point to yourself and then point to your eyes Last but not least, rock your child in your arms and enjoy.

Beautiful	měi lì
Sky	tiān kōng
Appear	chū lái
Shiny	guāng liàng de
Stars	xīng xīng
Mommy	mā ma
Loving	cí ài de
Eyes	yǎn jīng

Picnic (#24)

Zǒu zǒu zǒu zǒu zǒu
走 走 走 走 走
Walk, walk, walk, walk walk

Wǒ men xiǎo shǒu lā xiǎo shǒu
我 们 小 手 拉 小 手
Our small hands holding hands

Zǒu zǒu zǒu zǒu zǒu
走 走 走 走 走
Walk, walk, walk, walk, walk

Yì tóng qù jiāo yóu
一 同 去 郊 游
Together go on a picnic

Picnic	jiāo yóu
Walk	zǒu
Little hands	xiǎo shǒu
Hold hands	lā shǒu
Together	yì tóng
Go	qù

Teacher Tip

This is a great song that you can use to teach action words. You can teach the verb "zǒu"(walk) by singing the word "zǒu" to the melody of this song and demonstrating the action. Next try another verb like "tiào" (jump), and so on.

This is a perfect song to sing while walking and holding your child's hand. My daughter and I often sing this song while walking hand in hand to her preschool class. And my son happens to be learning to play this song on the piano. This is a popular song in our family!

The More We Get Together (#25)

Dāng wǒ men tóng zài yì qǐ
当 我 们 同 在 一 起
When we get together,

Here is a Mandarin Chinese version of the very well-known song!

Zài yì qǐ zài yì qǐ
在 一 起, 在 一 起
Together, together

Dāng wǒ men tóng zài yì qǐ
当 我 们 同 在 一 起
When we get together

Qí kuài lè wú bǐ
其 快 乐 无 比
How happy beyond compare

Nǐ duì zhe wǒ xiào xī xi
你 对 着 我 笑 嘻 嘻
You face me and laugh "xi xi"

Wǒ duì zhe nǐ xiào hā ha
我 对 着 你 笑 哈 哈
I face you and laugh "ha ha"

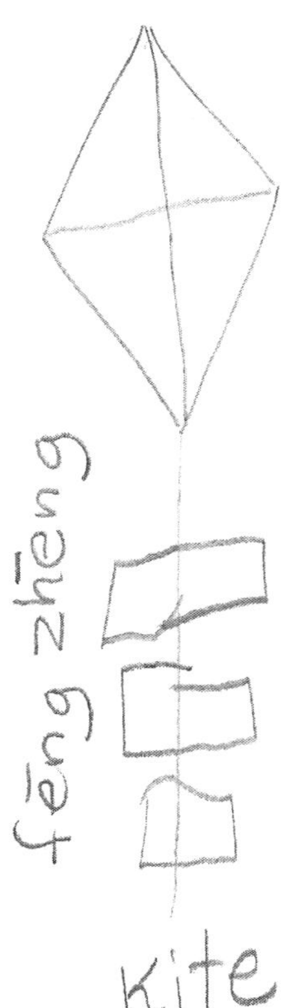

(The rest of the song continues on the next page.)

Dāng wǒ men tóng zài yì qǐ
当 我 们 同 在 一 起
When we get together,

Qí kuài lè wú bǐ
其 快 乐 无 比
How happy beyond compare

We	wǒ men
Get together	tóng zài yì qǐ
You face me	nǐ duì zhe wǒ
Laugh, smile	xiào
Happy	kuài lè

Teacher Tip

I like teaching this song because it has a ¾ time signature. First I use some instruments to demonstrate a 1-2-3 rhythm. Next we sing this song with the instruments keeping tempo. We also walk around the room in a circle to the 1-2-3 beat. Older children can do a waltzing step of "step (first count) and then up up" (second and third counts) on their tiptoes. You can carry your little ones while waltzing and let them feel the rhythm in their bodies.

Twinkle, Twinkle, Little Star (#26)

Yì shǎn yì shǎn liàng jīng jīng
一 闪 一 闪 亮 晶 晶
Twinkle, twinkle, shining bright

Mǎn tiān dōu shì xiǎo xīng xīng
满 天 都 是 小 星 星
All the sky is little stars

Guà zài tiān shàng fàng guāng míng
挂 在 天 上 放 光 明
Hanging up in the sky giving off light

Hǎo xiàng xǔ duō xiǎo yǎn jīng
好 像 许 多 小 眼 睛
Like many little eyes

Yì shǎn yì shǎn liàng jīng jīng
一 闪 一 闪 亮 晶 晶
Twinkle, twinkle, shining bright

Mǎn tiān dōu shì xiǎo xīng xīng
满 天 都 是 小 星 星
All the sky is little stars

Teacher Tip

Since this tune is so familiar, you can repeat the first two lines (or even just the first line) over and over again to the melody of the song until you can learn all the words.

Twinkle	yì shǎn
Bright	liàng
Shining	jīng jīng
Full	mǎn
Sky	tiān
All	dōu
Is	shì
Little	xiǎo
Stars	xīng xīng
Hang	guà
Give off	fàng
Bright light	guāng míng
Like	hǎo xiàng
Many	xǔ duō
Eyes	yǎn jīng

Two Tigers (#27)

Liǎng zhī lǎo hǔ (2X)
两 只 老 虎
Two tigers

Pǎo de kuài (2X)
跑 得 快
Run fast

Yì zhī méi yǒu ěr duo
一 只 没 有 耳 朵
One doesn't have an ear

Yì zhī méi yǒu wěi ba
一 只 没 有 尾 巴
One doesn't have a tail

Zhēn qí guài (2X)
真 奇 怪
How very strange!

Tiger	lǎo hǔ
Run fast	pǎo de kuài
No ear	méi yǒu ěr duo
No tail	méi yǒu wěi ba
Strange	qí guài

Where Is My Friend? (#28)

Yī èr sān sì wǔ liù qī
一 二 三 四 五 六 七
One, two, three, four, five, six, seven

Wǒ de péng yǒu zài nǎ lǐ
我 的 朋 友 在 哪 里
Where is my friend?

Zài zhè lǐ zài zhè lǐ
在 这 里, 在 这 里
Over here, over here

Wǒ de péng yǒu zài zhè lǐ
我 的 朋 友 在 这 里
My friend is right here!

Teacher Tip

I use this song to practice the sentence patterns __ zài nǎ lǐ (where is__) and __ zài zhè lǐ (__ is here).

These are really great phrases to use when playing Hide and Seek!

My	wǒ de
Friend	péng yǒu
At	zài
Where	nǎ lǐ
Here	zhè lǐ
Is	shì
You	nǐ

Frequently Used Vocabulary

Greetings and Phrases

Welcome	huān yíng
Hello	nǐ hǎo
Thank You	xiè xie
You're welcome	bú kè qì
Good morning	zǎo ān
Good bye	zài jiàn
My name is....	wǒ jiào ____(name)
How old are you?	nǐ jǐ suì
I am __ years old	wǒ___ suì (number)
My name is....	wǒ jiào ____(name)
See you next week	xià gè lǐ bài jiàn
I love you	wǒ ài nǐ

Pronouns

I	wǒ	我
You	nǐ	你
He	tā	他
She	tā	她
We, us	wǒ men	我 们
You (plural)	nǐ men	你 们
They, them	tā men	他 们

Numbers

One	yī	一
Two	èr	二
Three	sān	三
Four	sì	四
Five	wǔ	五
Six	liù	六
Seven	qī	七
Eight	bā	八
Nine	jiǔ	九
Ten	shí	十
Eleven	shí yī	十一
Twelve	shí èr	十二
Thirteen	shí sān	十三
Fourteen	shí sì	十四
Fiftenn	shí wǔ	十五
Sixteen	shí liù	十六
Seventeen	shí qī	十七
Eighteen	shí bā	十八
Nineteen	shí jiǔ	十九
Twenty	èr shí	二十
Thirty	sān shí	三 十
Forty	sì shí	四十
Fifty	wǔ shí	五 十
Hundred	yī bǎi	一 百

Parts of the Body

Head	tóu			头		
Eye	yǎn	jīng		眼	睛	
Nose	bí	zi		鼻	子	
Mouth	kǒu			口		
Mouth	zuǐ	bā		嘴	巴	
Ear	ěr	duo		耳	朵	
Shoulders	jiān	bǎng		肩	膀	
Hand	shǒu			手		
Leg	tuǐ			腿		
Foot	jiǎo			脚		
Knees	xī	gài		膝	盖	
Finger	shǒu	zhǐ	tou	手	指	头
Stomach	dù	zi		肚	子	
Bottom	pì	gǔ		屁	股	
Toes	jiǎo	zhǐ		脚	趾	

Colors

Color	yán	sè		颜	色	
White	bái	sè		白	色	
Black	hēi	sè		黑	色	
Red	hóng	sè		红	色	
Pink	fěn	hóng	sè	粉	红	色
Yellow	huáng	sè		黄	色	
Blue	lán	sè		蓝	色	
Orange	chéng	sè		橙	色	
Green	lǜ	sè		绿	色	
Purple	zǐ	sè		紫	色	

Action Words (Verbs)

Walk	zǒu	走
Run	pǎo	跑
Jump	tiào	跳
Dance	tiào wǔ	跳 舞
Sit	zuò	坐
Sit down	zuò xià lái	坐 下 来
Stand	zhàn	站
Stand up	zhàn qǐ lái	站 起 来
Kick	tī	踢
Fly	fēi	飞
Swim	yóu yǒng	游 泳
Clap hands	pāi pāi shǒu	拍 拍 手
Nod head	yáo yáo tóu	摇 摇 头
Shake hands	wò wò shǒu	握 握 手
Salute	jìng gè lǐ	敬 个 礼
Sleep	shuì jiào	睡 觉
Wake up	qǐ chuáng	起 床
Turn	zhuǎn yi zhuǎn	转 一 转
Put back	fàng huí qù	放 回 去

Direction Words

Up	shàng	上
Above	shàng miàn	上 面
Down	xià	下
Below	xià miàn	下 面
Front	qián miàn	前 面
Behind	hòu miàn	后 面
Left	zuǒ	左
Left side	zuǒ biān	左 边
Right	yòu	右
Right side	yòu biān	右 边

Animals

Cat	māo	猫
Dog	gǒu	狗
Mouse	lǎo shǔ	老 鼠
Tiger	lǎo hǔ	老 虎
Monkey	hóu zi	猴 子
Bird	niǎo	鸟
Sheep	yáng	羊
Chicken	jī	鸡
Pig	zhū	猪
Frog	qīng wā	青 蛙
Rabbit	tù zi	兔 子
Bear	xióng	熊
Panda	xióng māo	熊 猫

Pinyin Pronunciation Guide

Pinyin is a system that transliterates Mandarin Chinese into the Roman alphabet. The following chart provides the English equivalents of most of the sounds used in Chinese. The examples below are not perfect, but I think they come close.

Pinyin Notation	English Equivalent
b	b as in boy
p	p as in pal
m	m as in man
f	f as in fish
d	d as in dad
t	t as in ten
n	n as in nice
l	l as in love
g	g as in girl
k	k as in kid
h	h as in he
j	j as in jeep
q	"ch" as in chest
x	she
zh	like the j in junk
ch	like the "ch" in church

Pinyin	English Equivalent	Notes
sh	"sh" as in shirt	
r	like the r in leisure	
z	like the s in reads	
c	like the s in hats	
s	like the s in socks	
y	y as in yes	

w	w as in water	
	The following are vowel sounds and endings:	
a	"a" as in father	
o	oh	
e	British "e" in her	Like "uh" in "what"
i	Listen for the "i" sound in the word "zhi" at the beginning of " Frog Song" (#6 on the CD)	after z,c,s,zh, ch, sh,r
i	"ee"	after other consonants
u	"oo"	after most letters
u	like saying "ee" with round lips	after n, l, j, q, x , y
ai	eye	
ei	eight	
ao	"ow" as in now	
ou	oh	
er	"er"	
an	on	
en	like the "ur" in British "turn"	
ang	like the "ong" in song	
eng	like the "ung" in sung	
ong	"ohng"	
ia	like the "ia" in Asia	
ie	like the "ye" in yes	
iao	like "eow" in meow	
iu	"eo" as in Leo	but as one syllable
ian	"ee-yen"	one syllable

iang	"ee-yahng"	one syllable
in	"een" as in green	
ua	like the "ua" in guava	
uo	like the o in the New York English pronunciation of c*o*ffee	
ui	way	
un	say "ee" with round lips followed by the "n" sound	after j, q, and x
uai	like the "wi" in wi-fi" preceded by "oo"	one syllable

Four Tones in Chinese

There are four tones in Chinese plus a neutral tone. Words with the same sound have different meanings depending on the tone. Tone markings are above the vowel in Hanyu Pinyin notation. Please see the following chart:

Tone markings for the sound "Ma"

Tone	Marking	How It Sounds
1	Mā	High and flat tone, level sound
2	Má	Tone rises from middle
3	Mǎ	Tone dips down and then rises up
4	Mà	Tone falls from high to low
Neutral	Ma	Light tone with no emphasis

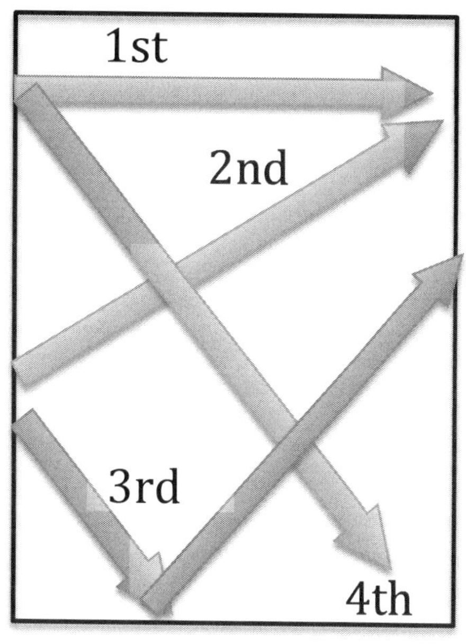

The graph to the left shows the relative pitch of each tone.

Credits

Book:

Graphic Artist:	May Yeung
Illustrators:	Seraphine Chen, Moses Chen, Jim Chen
Chinese Editors:	Xiao Qing Chen and Joy Chung
English Editor:	Emily Liu (Introduction and Back Cover)
Publishing Editor:	Steven Chen

Music CD:

Vocalists:	Seraphine Chen, Moses Chen Steven Chen, Patricia Tina Wu
Instrumentalists:	
Flute:	Jenny Robinet
Harp:	Peter Huang
Percussion:	Seraphine and Moses Chen
Piano:	Erica Huang ("Picnic" and "The More We Get Together")
Piano:	Patricia Tina Wu
Violin:	Lizzy Robinet
Other Instruments:	Patricia Tina Wu

Acknowledgements

Thank you, Jane Emery, for believing in this project from the outset. I know you are still cheering me on.

Thank you to my students (and their parents) who have given me the opportunity to try out all my ideas, and who have been patient through all the flops. Thank you, Karis Academy, for being such a warm and creative environment. It's every teacher's dream place to teach. Thanks, especially, to Karis' Director, Wendy Lee, for your unwavering support.

Thank you, Julie Wong, from Music Around the World. You first trained me to teach music and second language together and opened my eyes to its amazing possibilities.

Thank you, May, for your graphic design prowess and for your friendship. You were so gracious to agree to design a book cover for a "little" project that ended up involving an entire year of asking for your help, time and advice. You are an amazing artist. Thank you for everything.

Thank you to all my musicians, for being willing to give so generously of your talents and time, and for being willing to record and re-record so many times.

Thank you, Xiao Qing and Joy, for your tireless editing of my Chinese, pinyin, and translations; and for being willing to look at my drafts through the countless revisions.

Thank you, Emily, for looking over my English with your professorial eyes and for your encouraging words.

Thank you, Tina, for your honest opinion, your language expertise and for asking me what my next goal is.

Thank you, Cammie, for your very practical suggestions.

Thank you to my girlfriends for all your love, prayers, advice and input on the book. Thanks for joining me on this journey.

Thank you, Mom and Dad, for supporting my artistic endeavors with the birthday money.

Thank you to Minna for the legal advice and to Florin and Jessica for your experienced business perspectives.

Thanks, Babi, for the excellent illustrations. They are good!

Thank you, Moses and Seraphine, for being my students from birth and for cooperating with Mommy's crazy ideas.

Thank you, Moses, for singing and reciting so well, for your sophisticated drawings and for your expert eyes and ears.

Thank you, Seraphine, for your adorable drawings, for your lovely voice, and for being so patient and mature through the many recordings and re-recordings. You are a great singer!

And finally, thank you so much, Steve, for standing with me all these years, resolving all my technical problems, talking things out with me, staying up all hours of the night helping me, spending all those hours with my laptop at Starbucks during Chinese school, for diffusing my frustrations, telling me to keep going, singing for the recordings, and taking the kids on all the outings so I could stay home and work on this project. You are truly my biggest support. It's finally done. We did it!! ☺

CD Song List

1. Numbers 1-20
2. Colors
3. Body Parts
4. Big Head (p. 4)
5. Frog Song (p. 5)
6. Frying Eggs (p. 6)
7. Little Leather Ball (p. 7)
8. Little Mouse (p. 9)
9. Little White Cat (p. 11)
10. Still Night (p. 12)
11. Butterfly (p. 14)
12. Counting Song (p. 15)
13. Drop the Handkerchief (p. 16)
14. Elephant (p. 18)
15. Fast Train (p. 19)
16. Firefly (p. 21)
17. Grandma's Bridge (p. 22)
18. Harp Lullaby (p. 23)
19. Head, Shoulders, Knees, and Toes (p. 24)
20. Little Sister Carries a Doll (p. 25)
21. Little Swallow (p.27)
22. Looking for a Friend (p.28)
23. Mommy's Eyes (p.29)
24. Picnic (p.30)
25. The More We Get Together (p.31)
26. Twinkle, Twinkle, Little Star (p.33)
27. Two Tigers (p.35)
28. Where Is My Friend? (p.36)